THE
PROTESTANT
AND
POLITICS

LAYMAN'S THEOLOGICAL LIBRARY
ROBERT McAFEE BROWN, *General Editor*

The
Protestant
and
Politics

by
William Lee Miller

LAYMAN'S
THEOLOGICAL
LIBRARY

THE WESTMINSTER PRESS

PHILADELPHIA

Library of Congress Catalog Card No. 58–8256

PRINTED IN THE UNITED STATES OF AMERICA

Contents

The religious book market is full of books for "the intelligent layman." Some are an insult to his intelligence. Others are covertly written for professional theologians. A few are genuine helps in communicating the faith.

In this spate of books being thrust at the lay reader, what distinctive place can the Layman's Theological Library claim to hold? For one thing, it will try to remind the layman that he *is* a theologian. The close conjunction of the words "layman" and "theological" in the title of the series is not by chance but by design. For theology is not an irrelevant pastime of seminary professors. It is the occupation of every Christian, the moment he begins to think about, or talk about, or communicate, his Christian faith. The injunction to love God *with all his mind,* necessarily involves the layman in theology. He can never avoid theology; if he refuses to think through his faith, he simply settles for an inferior theology.

Furthermore, the Layman's Theological Library will attempt to give a *wholeness* in its presentation of the Christian faith. Its twelve volumes cover the main areas of Christian faith and practice. They are written out of similar convictions which the authors share about the uniqueness of the Christian faith. All the authors are convinced that Christian faith can be made relevant, that it can be made understandable without becoming

9

innocuous, and that (particularly in view of the current " return to religion ") it is crucially important for the layman to commit himself to more than " religion in general." The Layman's Theological Library, then, will attempt a fresh exploration of the Christian faith and what it can mean in the life of twentieth-century man.

There have always been people who have echoed one of the complaints with which this book tries to deal, namely, that " religion and politics don't mix."

Pharaoh didn't like Moses "meddling" with the way he ran Egypt, and he certainly didn't like Moses " upsetting the economy " by his pleading for the Israelite slaves. The Old Testament prophets from Amos and Isaiah on down got pretty rough treatment when they suggested that there was a word from the Lord that challenged the political and economic life of the people, and challenged it in radical terms. One of the charges against Jesus was that he threatened the stability of the Roman Empire and its strangle hold on downtrodden peoples like the Jews. Whatever else his death represents (and it represents a great deal more), it represents in part the attempt of the Roman Empire to get rid of someone who was fast becoming a political nuisance.

Calvin, Knox, and all the Reformers got into difficulty themselves when they discovered that to take the Christian faith with full seriousness meant that full involvement in political life, political decisions, and political responsibility was inevitable. And in our own day, German pastors, for example, have discovered that to preach Jesus Christ means preaching about the political and economic situation in which their congregations live. They have also discovered that the people who control the political and economic situation — whether nazi or communist — take a very dim view of this sort of thing, with the result that a great many German pastors have had to answer with their lives for speaking with such boldness.

Such extreme reactions as this don't happen to prevail very widely in the United States at the moment, although there are a good many Christians in various parts of the country who have recently discovered that to suggest that God " made of one blood all nations of men," is to court threatening phone calls and bombs thrown through living room windows.

Apparently one of the reasons people keep on insisting that "religion and politics don't mix" is that they are not at all sure they will like the result that emerges from the mixing. And they have a right to be perturbed. For there is nothing quiescent or static about a situation when it really begins to be scrutinized in the light of the full Christian gospel. The times of greatest vitality in the history of Christian faith have been the times when it was recognized as a revolutionary faith, as a faith that made demands, that challenged " the way things are," that upset the neat patterns men had imposed upon their common life together.

So there is some justification for being a bit alarmed when anybody suggests that, for example, " the Protestant and politics" belong together. But one's reaction to such a proposal becomes a pretty clear indication of where his ultimate loyalties lie. The person whose ultimate loyalty lies with " the way things are " will naturally object if Christian faith starts muscling in and invading his territory. The person whose ultimate loyalty is given to God will see, in the light of that loyalty, that every other concern must be judged, appraised, re-evaluated and changed in the light of who God is and what he demands of his people.

But this kind of talk can remain very theoretical and eso-teric unless there is someone around to bring it down to earth and supply the concerned Christian with some of the ground rules, some of the information, and some of the plain know-how for translating his faith into active political responsibility. In bridging that gap — one of the widest gaps contemporary Christians have to face — the present book can be of inestimable help.

ROBERT McAFEE BROWN

THE AMERICAN PRESENT

This is a book about Christianity and politics, but it does not treat that imposing subject in the abstract, addressed to whom it may concern. It deals with American politics; the Christians to whom it addresses itself are American Protestants; and the time with which it is concerned is the present.

The present furnishes some of the reasons for treating this subject; the nature of Christianity furnishes others. We begin with the former. We begin, not with Protestant principles, or doctrine, or the Biblical view; we begin instead where Christian doctrine says we may begin, where Protestantism did begin, and where the Bible does begin: with the specific situation of men in a particular time and place — our own.

And our own time differs radically, not only from that of the Bible, but also from that of a century ago, when the political mind of American Protestantism took shape, or even from that of a few short years ago.

Take two examples.

1. *Life among the organizations.* One hundred years ago in the United States there were few big corporations or big businesses, practically no labor unions, trade associations, or farm organizations, no American Legion, no Department of Labor or of Agriculture, and a federal government infinitesimal by

modern standards. Most people worked for themselves; the lawyer hung out his shingle, the doctor was the general practitioner for the town, the local church, the school, the family farm, the general store were centers of life.

Since then there has been what Kenneth Boulding calls the "organizational revolution." We now live with General Motors, General Foods, and General Electric; with the Teamsters, the Machinists, and the Steam Fitters; with the Steel Workers and the Auto Workers; with the Apple Growers and the Beet Growers, the Milk Producers and the National Livestock Association; with the NBC that has radio shows and the NBC that makes biscuits; with the American Petroleum Institute, the American Cotton Manufacturers Association, the American Iron and Steel Institute; with the CAA and the NCAA, the AAA and the other AAA; with the UAW, the AMA, the NAM, the FHA, the NLRB, the ILGWU, the ORO, the ABPA, the N.F. of A. (I just made up the last ones, but I dare say they represent something somewhere.)

New machines create great new centers of power. Two hundred largest corporations own one fourth of America's national wealth. General Motors Corporation could buy everything — every house, blade of grass, and shoestring — in the states of Kansas, Nebraska, and Wyoming, and a couple of others thrown in for good measure.

Along with great concentration of power there is also a great leveling. We all come home and eat the same brands of food, watch the same television shows, discuss the same subjects treated by the same magazines.

We live in an age of vast assembly lines, giant corporations, huge office buildings, vast and sprawling suburbs of vast and sprawling cities. We live with crowded subways, crowded movie theaters, crowded highways, crowded supermarkets, crowded schools. Main Street has given way to the Jersey Turnpike, Abilene to Levittown; the town meeting and the band concert have been replaced by the world news roundup and Perry Como.

The past, in which the political ideas of Americans (and especially those of Protestantism) were shaped, is fading fast.

This is what has happened: *one of the most individualistic nations in the world has become one of the most massively organized of all.*

2. *Life among the nations.* One hundred years ago our experience of the clash of nations was even less developed than our experience of the clash of organizations. The budget then for foreign affairs would hardly keep the Pentagon in light bulbs today. The United States of America had been formed with the idea that it had left behind the power politics, the wars, the imperialism, and the diplomatic maneuverings of those tired, old nations of Europe. We thought that we would live our own life in our own part of the globe, demonstrating democracy to the world, but not having any "foreign entanglements."

But now we are entangled as no nation was ever entangled before in foreign entanglements.

We are allied in one way or another with forty-two nations, in alliances like NATO, SEATO, OAS; we have bases in Iceland, Saudi Arabia, Morocco, Greenland, in countries around the world; we have given, in foreign aid, some forty billion dollars (much more than the entire Federal expenditure for the decade of the 1920's); we are members of the UN, the WHO, the ILO, the ICAO.

Minor decisions about tariffs on fish in Washington have a major repercussion on the economy of Japan and Iceland.

Our power affects people everywhere; our cars and Coca-Cola and jazz circle the globe; our actions are watched, our purposes examined, our errors feared.

Most important of all, in the bombers of our Strategic Air Command, in our nuclear stock pile, and in our missiles, we hold the power that can plunge the world into all-out nuclear war — or that may deter the Russians from acts that would bring it on.

This is what has happened: *one of the most isolated of nations has suddenly become the most deeply involved of all.*

The Power of the American Public

And who is it that shapes the decisions in this impressive age of nuclear weapons and massive organization? You, gentle reader, and I. It is true that a few men in offices in New York and Washington have immense power — but they have it within limits set by our attitudes. They act with one eye cocked to the reaction of that rich, mysterious, powerful, erratic, moody being, " the American public."

That public is rich. The United States, with 5 per cent of the world's people, has half of the world's wealth; the other 95 per cent of all human beings has to be content with the other half.

And it is powerful. Four fifths of the people of the world either never had, or have lost, the power to influence the course of the world events. Seven hundred million people living in Russia and her satellites are controlled by a thorough and ruthless dictatorship. The majority of the people of the world live under governments that never have given them real democratic control, as in Asia and in much of Africa and Latin America. The capacity of the older democracies in Europe to control the events of the world has greatly diminished. The place where people generally have a major effect upon the course of world events is in the United States.

About Politics

But — this is part of the problem — in the United States people generally do not think very much, or very well, about the politics this new age requires.

Before we go any farther, let's say what we mean by that word "politics." We mean the fight for power wherever it is, not only the struggle of East and West in the disarmament conferences, and of Republicans and Democrats for offices in Washington and the City Hall, but also office politics, union politics, farm politics, and (don't forget this) church politics.

Decisions have to be made. Unfortunately, we cannot have a cake and eat it too. There's only so much land, so much water, so much oil; only one person can be President, one party a majority; what's spent for the church building can't be spent for benevolences; what's plowed back into capital expansion can't be given to the stockholders in dividends; what's spent in foreign aid can't be returned in lower income taxes; we cannot vote both no and yes in the United Nations General Assembly; a throughway has to go in one place or another; the bomb (that may spread radioactive fall-out over Nevada, but may teach something we need to know) has to be set off or held back.

There are differences about what decision should be made. Some people are Republicans, some Democrats; some are aided by inflation, some hurt; some are landlords, some are renters; some are conservatives, some liberals; some middle of the road, some left, some right, some out in the field; some segregationists, some integrationists; some like it hot, some like it cold, some like it . . . well, you get the idea.

Politics is the struggle over these decisions on which people differ, by groups. It is the conflict over the ability to make the decisions — that is, over power.

America's Attempt to Escape from Politics

We Americans now have a lot of that power; but power or politics is not really our best field. Someone has written that there is more intelligence displayed by an eighteen-year-old American boy fixing his Ford than by the United States Senate debating foreign policy.

We are much better at problems that are tangible (Fords) than with those in which there are many intangibles (foreign policy).

Why is this?

Because our idealism and our individualism, and also our good fortune, have made us that way.

We have had a great trust that ideals can be made real in the society; we've believed that American know-how can master foreign policy as it can manufacture Fords; we've assumed that by rousing energy the world could be made over — and we've been impatient with the politics that always seems quite a comedown from the idealist's vision.

We have also believed in individual success. We are a nation that teaches its children that there is room at the top and that one can get ahead. This centering upon private success means that we do not have a very sturdy tradition of public responsibility (though it's often celebrated in a rather uninteresting way in high school civics classes and Fourth-of-July oratory). The economic philosophy we inherited said that if every man pursued his own private financial advancement, the over-all problems of the public would take care of themselves (but they don't).

It is not only our ideals that have made us miss our political lessons; our fortunate life has helped. We've been fortunate to have a working two-party system — a system that can exist because we don't have political extremes, and one that keeps these extremes from growing. We've not had deep divisions over land reform, over ancient hereditary property rights, and over stark poverty of whole classes of people.

We've been fortunate in the immense productivity of our economy, which has meant that we've been able to overcome a lot of problems, not by solving them politically, but with immense expansion of production of goods. In a way, we've dodged the questions that countries with scarcity have had to fight out.

We've become fascinated by and brilliant in the technical ability (know-how) that works better in building bridges than it does in making friends in the Middle East.

We've had so much elbowroom that we haven't had to notice how much of life is a struggle for elbowroom. When the struggle comes out in the open in politics we look down our noses at it, not seeing that the struggle is a part of life everywhere — in business, in social life, even in the family — and the area we call "politics" is not really any dirtier than these.

As a result, we have a considerable nonpolitical and even an antipolitical tradition. The word "politics" itself has negative overtones. "Power politics" is especially a derogatory phrase, and a joke like Ambrose Bierce's ("I'm not a politician, and my other habits are good") reflects a standard attitude. Men can be elected in the United States in part because they are *not* politicians, and because they are thought to be "above politics." Politics is seen to be an ugly realm of scheming, of calculation, of compromise, of general nastiness.

But this is what has happened: *a nation with a most unpolitical tradition has now become the nation that most urgently needs political understanding.*

The Protestant and Politics

Now, what of American Protestantism?

It has shared the American's idealism and individualism, and it has shared the American's negative attitude toward politics — in fact, it helped to create them.

We Protestants can be proud of many things our heritage has given to the spirit of America, but that negative attitude toward politics is not one of them.

We need citizens who think well about politics; Protestantism serves us badly if it tends to discourage rather than to encourage such citizens.

Fortunately, there are resources in Protestant faith and theology for overcoming its own defects — including, first, that fundamental defect, the idea that religion and politics have no connection. Let's start with that.

About Mixing and Meddling

When we hear a talk about "religion and politics" at a church supper, it probably goes something like this:

"We think politics is dirty, but it is made dirty partly by the good people who stay out. The Bible is concerned with social affairs. Amos insists that justice should roll down as waters, and that the poor should not be sold as sandals. Jesus prays, 'Thy kingdom come on earth.' Jesus and the Bible have harsh words for the rich, the proud, the mighty, whose hypocritical worship the Lord despises, because it does not issue in justice. Christians should not identify Christianity with any particular program, but should seek out political programs that most nearly express their Christianity."

This is a good speech; many of us have heard it, and some of us have made it, a lot of times. But as we sit in the fellowship hall listening to it again, perhaps some questions now occur to us. As we look out over the group sitting, eating their meat loaf and coleslaw, listening to the exhortation to "get into politics," and we think of all of them trooping down the next morning to some ward headquarters — if they find it — to enroll as Christians on the side of morality and justice, all at once we wonder whether politics, widely known to be dirty, would really be washed clean by this sturdy delegation from First Church. Maybe it would go on being rather dirty after all, and maybe some of the leaders of the church would be involved in the dirtiness.

Or maybe the parishioners' earnest effort at cleaning up would cause more trouble than it was worth! Why? Because they would be filled with those antipolitical notions that are quite out of touch with the realities of the present we talked about — and out of touch, too, with most of historic Christian truth. The most basic of these notions is the one that separates politics from the ultimate questions of religion.

Let's listen to some standard American objections to religion in politics at the church supper — and to the response of the speechmaker.

First, the opponents say (growing, perhaps, a little red in the face) that religion shouldn't " meddle " (that is the word, isn't it?) in politics; they insist that religion and politics should not mix.

But the speaker (well read in theological series like this one) knows the answer to that: religion, he says, is not just one compartment of life, alongside of, separated from, others; religion — or the Christian religion, anyway — is not one room of life, but the foundation of all the rooms of life and, therefore, related to all of them. It deals not with a segment but with the center, and from the center should come the motive and the insight for the whole.

Part of the case of the objectors would be more or less *theological,* though they might be a little startled to hear it described that way. "Religion is a *private* matter," they would say. "Its business is with the *spiritual life,* not with worldly affairs; it deals with *individuals,* not with institutions; it is concerned with *saving souls,* not with politics."

But the speaker's answer to this is clear too: what these phrases represent is not the Christian religion but a popular and modern thing, individualistic and pseudospiritual, the product of the compartmentalizing of life mentioned before. As for Christianity, *just because* it is truly and deeply concerned with individual souls, it has *therefore* necessarily been concerned with the institutions that shape their lives. Christianity is not a religion about some "spiritual" realm in heaven or a "private" realm, a Kingdom of God within you, underneath your collar bone or something; it does not make a sharp separation between the "spiritual" and the "material"; there is no negation of the public world in favor of some private nonmaterial existence. The temporal world, including politics, is made *more* important, not less, by the doctrines of Christian faith, which affirm that God created the world, that the Word became flesh, that God acts to reconcile the world to himself.

But what of the Constitution? say the debaters. It establishes the separation of church and state.

So it does, replies our champion. But separating the institutions of church and state does *not* mean separating the religious conscience from politics — that's something quite different, and a bad idea.

Well, say the opponents, we must "begin with the individuals," and if we convert every individual, then social problems "will take care of themselves." The church should convert individuals and "leave them to apply Christian principles in politics on their own."

Unfortunately, says the speaker, this usually means they are not applied, particularly not where it hurts. Just suppose, he might reply, thinking in good pastoral style of an example, that the good Samaritan coming along the road, letting "everything else take care of itself," had been so intent on his meditations on the Kingdom of God within him that he had not seen the man lying wounded and robbed at the side of the road.

Would we not say that there was something deficient in that faith?

Now take another step, says the speaker. Suppose the good Samaritan came upon the wounded man and took him to the inn and cared for him, and then came the next day and found another man in the same condition, and dealt again with his wounds in the same way. Then suppose that on the next day and the next he met wounded travelers at the same place beside the same road, that he helped and cared for each of them. Suppose this went on for weeks.

Would we not think that there was something deficient in his faith if he never thought to ask who was patrolling that road against bandits?

Suppose he were a person of power in the community. Would there not be something deficient in the faith that never thought to use that power to try to prevent the attacks on travelers?

What if the servant of God would give his last bread to a starving stranger in a bread line, yet never think to ask questions about the economic conditions that cause the bread line to exist?

Another objection to religion-in-politics — perhaps the more compelling part — may sound something like this: " What do you want, churches divided along party lines? If religion meddles in politics, then all sorts of worldly differences of opinion are brought into the church; congregations shrink, there is division and conflict in the church, and religious ideas are forgotten in political argument."

To this, our theological spokesman might answer that (granting all sorts of difficulties) still the maintaining of a large, harmonious, and inoffensive congregation is not really the first purpose of the church; that if problems matter enough for people to differ vigorously, then there is probably something worth talking about at stake.

Maybe, by this time, it is getting late, and it is almost time to thank the cooks (Mrs. Wilkins for the splendid meat loaf, Mrs. Johnson for the lovely coleslaw), to gather up wives and overshoes and make one's way home. But then the opponents of religion-in-politics think of their best argument, the one their theological opponent cannot answer so readily. Instead of talking about the damage politics can do to religion, they turn to the damage religion-in-practice can do to politics.

" When you get religion mixed into politics (or business or any public or practical life, for that matter) then things really get nasty: Protestants fight Catholics, Christians fight Jews, the church people fight the secularists, the community is divided, the Democrats say they are doing God's will; the Republicans say, no, *they* are doing God's will; people get filled with self-righteousness and moralism, interfering in things they don't know anything about, telling other people what's good for them, because they think they've got a direct pipeline to God — it's no good. Politics is separate from religion. Let's keep it that way."

What do we say to this? What do we say about all the fights and nastiness, all the fanaticism and holy wars, all the callous complacency, self-importance, and just plain pious ignorance that religion has helped to make in politics? The case for Christianity in politics may be fine in theory, but the results in practice often are appalling.

Shall we close up this book right here, call the whole thing off, and go on to safer subjects?

Let's make just this very modest case for going on: religion is going to be "mixed" in politics, one way or another, whether we like it or not. The only choice we really have is, What kind of mixture will it be? Let's work on that, and begin by admitting frankly the damage religion can do.

THE TROUBLE RELIGION CAN CAUSE IN POLITICS

Religion is widely recommended now as a Good Thing for American Democracy. This recommendation comes not only from clergymen (whose tendency to favor religion is well known) but also from college presidents, baseball players, corporation executives, Sunday magazine writers, and public officials, especially including Presidents of the United States. Religion is said to make us superior to the communists; it is said to be the " foundation " of our political system, the source of our national strength. Is it? Well, that depends, doesn't it? It depends on what kind of religion we mean, and it remains to be proved.

In this chapter, we have two big headings for the harm religion can do, with plenty of subtypes.

1. Religionism, Its Varieties, Its Cousins and Its Aunts

One of the most troublesome habits of religious people is that they tend to become very interested in religion.

This means, among other things, that " religion " is treated not as an enlargement of the dimensions of life, but as a separate and self-sufficient realm of its own. Then, either that realm displaces politics, or worse, takes it over, mixing the absolute and inclusive loyalties of religion with the relative and shifting loyalties of politics. Let's take a look at both of these dangers.

Manicuring spiritual fingernails

The first of them used to be represented by that old favorite, "pie in the sky by-and-by," but that pie is no longer alamode; now the otherworldliness of religion is represented less by harps, heaven, and an eternal reward beyond, and more by peace of mind, peace of soul, peace with God (anyway, peace) within — but the result is much the same. Men turn away from the world to some other separated domain of religion where they seek eternal bliss or inner serenity, while burly sinners rule the world.

The communists say that religion is an opiate of the people, giving men a dopey dream of bliss in another world to keep them from noticing the conditions of this. Sometimes they are right.

Religion may view the world from such an elevated peak that the hills and valleys of this world don't seem to be very important at all; the vast panorama of eternity may dwarf the little distinctions of politics, seeming to make them insignificant.

In times past, the church was counted upon by segregation's defenders to teach the Negro hymn-singing instead of political organization — to drain off in religious emotion the energies that might have gone into social protest.

In the last century a religious organization for railroad workers asked funds from railroad tycoons, pointing out that members of the organization, being tamed by religion, were less likely than other workers to strike.

The publishers of a best-selling "religious" book of recent years recommend that executives give it to their employees, because it quiets complaints, gives renewed faith in what they sell (apparently without regard to what that may be), and engenders uncritical enthusiasm for the firm.

However much men may want to separate religion and politics, religion does have a political effect — if only implicitly or inadvertently. To speak constantly about the highest and most important things, without ever turning critical attention to the surrounding society, teaches by implication either (*a*) that the arrangements of society are not important or (*b*) that the existing arrangements are hunky-dory. Plenty of religion has been content to leave that last impression.

The crusaders

But if religion can have bad effects when it ignores the political arena, it can have even worse effects when it pays attention to it! Here come the crusaders, their banners emblazoned with " religion," God on their side, a claim of absolute superiority over their opponents on their lips, and an unwillingness to understand or compromise with the other, infidel side in their hearts.

Religion extended into politics often lends its note of absoluteness to what are actually the very relative matters of politics.

This may happen on any side of the political warfare, making the reformer's causes and crusades more fanatical and self-righteous, or making the conservative's defense of his vested interests more smug and complacent. We will talk about the reformer, under another heading, in a moment. Just now let's pay attention to the conservative side.

Sanctifying the status quo

No instrument of the devil has been more effective than the identification of Christianity with the ideas of the people on the right side of the tracks. Protestantism has been around a long time in the United States; like majority religions elsewhere in the world it has become all mixed up with conservative opinions.

Serious and alert people are often kept outside the church by noticing that it is composed, not only of what Mark Twain called Good Men, in the worst sense of the word, but also of elders who own decrepit tenements, deacons who think foreigners and Jews are dirty, and trustees who expect the preacher to reflect exactly the suburban congregation's conservative political sentiments.

There lingers in the minds of many American Protestants a feeling that capitalism is God's plan, that radicals and socialists and such are by definition ungodly. The free market system is often spoken of, not as one useful and working alternative among others, but as a *natural law* of supply and demand, an inviolable intention of the Creator. Private property is regarded as an exclusive, God-given right, rather than one of the many possible ways people have arranged their societies.

The point of the last paragraphs is not necessarily to speak against these worthy institutions of capitalism; the point is simply to break the total identification between them and God's will. Some conservative American Christians have their American conservatism and their Christianity so intermingled that they can't understand the very large part of world Christianity that is socialist, or anyway not capitalist. (Many of the socialist Christians around the world lack understanding of American capitalism, too, by the way, but they're not the ones we're speaking to at the moment.) This inability to understand other positions is especially offensive (*a*) when we are rich, and (*b*) when we bring God into it.

" Courage, God, we come "

The most important and dangerous example of religionism has to do with our attitude toward communism. We speak continually of the " godless " Soviets with their " materialistic " philosophy of " atheistic " communism, and by implication, at least, we seem to make ourselves the godly, righteous, and sober agents of religion and spirituality against these agents of the devil. Sometimes this identification of ourselves with God and religion is not just implied but quite explicit, as when it is asserted that we must " preserve Christianity " against those who would " pull down God from the skies."

This attitude is terribly dangerous politically, and it is mistaken religiously. It is dangerous politically because it tends to create an absolute, black-and-white division between " us " and " them," and to infuse that division with the most uncompromising passions; it helps to create the spirit of a holy war, and it fills the cold war with a heightened emotion that makes its hard choices more difficult. This religious self-righteousness produces an unwillingness to acknowledge realities of communist power and control (as in China), and it leads continually into moralistic declarations against them (like " liberation " doctrine) that, when the chips are down, we are not willing to support. This inclination of Americans to treat the communist problem in a petulant mood of absolute ideological-religious condemnation is one of the evidences of the political immaturity we described in Chapter 1, and it worries the allies, who, as we also said in that chapter, are now heavily dependent upon us. Out of its impulsive, crusading attitude have come many mistakes, and they might end in thermonuclear suicide for the world.

But if seeing ourselves as God's defenders is bad politics, it is worse religion. Christianity is a faith that cannot genuinely become a tribal religion, or a divine endorsement of our side, or a spiritual weapon against opponents; the many times it seems to have been so, it has been counterfeit. The faith itself takes unexpected turns that upset those who try to use it that way. It asserts that the "good" people can do the worst things, that the "religious" people can be most irreligious, that those who know God can sin most deeply against him. The Pharisees, the good, religious folk filled to the brim with moral and spiritual values, are less justified, in their pride, than the sinful but contrite publicans. It is as true of religious awareness as of material possessions that from those to whom much is given, much will be required. "You only have I known of all the families of the earth," says God to his chosen ones through the prophet Amos. And he follows with the startling conclusion, "therefore I will punish you." It is no justification of the communists to say that, if we really want to talk of the world contest in religious terms, then the first questions must be asked of ourselves.

The separate realm of religion has many forms: it may appear as theological knowledge, which, instead of deepening political thinking, becomes a substitute for it; it may be a devotional interest that, instead of undergirding action in the world, discourages it; it may be a commitment to the organized church that, instead of raising the political level, lowers it.

Let's say a word about that last one.

A variety: churchly tribalism

Some Protestants seem to assume that they should support any Protestant against any Catholic, Jew, or atheist, apparently regardless of the political issues involved.

Or they decide political questions on the basis of the welfare of the Protestant institution. Not too long ago (1928), Protestant antagonism to Catholics was a major item in a presidential election; Al Smith, himself, thought it was the most important aspect of all in his defeat. Social prejudices were tangled with religious ones to make an ugly combination. Protestant Christianity was (and to a lesser extent still is) mixed up in the prejudices of old established sections, classes, and groups in this nation — against the city, the immigrant, the foreign-born, the man who worked at the Fulton fish market.

Protestant anti-Catholicism is not only part of this social snobbery; there is also a strictly religious element. Two questions may be asked about it:

Do Protestant attitudes here reflect the broad understanding their own faith would recommend — or a kind of stereotype, and defensiveness against a rival institution?

Are the issues dividing Protestant and Catholic really momentous — or are they, in a larger national view, minor?

It is a little hard to believe, in the age of the ICBM, that elections should turn on question of parochial school buses.

It does seem odd, in the age of automation, inflation, and integration, that the issue that should rouse Protestantism's most fervent response should be that of an ambassador to the Vatican.

Something does seem askew when the two great sections of Christianity appear to be more concerned with their mutual antagonism than with their common calling to deepen the spirit of the nation.

If we should again have a Catholic nominee for national office, it would be a real test of the maturity of American Protestantism.

2. Morals, Motives, Principles, Good Men, and All That

We have spoken of the confusion caused by religion as " religion "; now we note the further confusion it causes through its local agent for worldly problems, " morality."

If the reader has ever read a textbook in " ethics," he probably will remember how the discussion kept heading out to sea or off into the woods: " There were three men on a desert island, but food enough for only one and a half . . ."; " Somebody had to be thrown out of the lifeboat . . ."; " This man alone with him in the woods was his friend as a person, but an enemy spy. . . ." (Did you hear about Sam? He went on his world tour with a splendid set of solutions to problems on desert islands and lifeboats but, worse luck, the ship never sank!)

The reason writers on ethics head for the island is plain: they want to isolate, for academic purposes, the purely moral element of problems. But then the temptation is to stay out there, to think that a moral principle remains isolated. It does not. It especially does not in politics. One principle must be related to other, contradictory principles, and all principles must be related to an understanding of the existing situation.

An example: Pacifists sometimes argue as though the non-pacifist hadn't quite grasped the point that peace is good and war is terrible. But that point cannot be separated from others (that tyranny and oppression are also terrible) or from an understanding of the real results that a course of action will produce in the world (the pacifist's rejection of the military balance against the enemy may really help to bring on the war the pacifist intends to reject).

The choice that is clear on the island is *not* clear on the ship, because other choices crowd in. The nonmoral considerations multiply. Things get complicated. This is true enough in face-to-face relations, but overwhelmingly so in politics. There, everything turns, not on your answer to some purely moral questions, but on how you define the situation for yourself. "Do justice, though the heavens fall." Well, what's justice? Which heavens are going to be allowed to fall? Men who talk a great deal about "morality" and "righteousness" in politics usually bootleg in with these terms their own particular (and limited) idea of the situation. Sometimes it seems that all "morality" does is to add a touch of self-righteousness to their doing what they were going to do anyway.

Unspotted from the world

One way churchfolk head for that moral island is by over-emphasizing motives, intentions, inner purity — especially, their own. There's good Biblical precedent for that emphasis; in their hearts, and in heaven, all Christians must come back to it — but we aren't yet in heaven, and all the important transactions are not in the heart. Politics deals with something short of the ultimate situation Jesus spoke about. It may be that lust in the heart is ultimately and morally as bad as lust put into action, but, meanwhile, here on earth, there is a considerable social difference between them!

The moral man often seems to think that it is more important for him to remain right and pure than for some concrete improvement to be made in the world.

Bernard Shaw wrote: "Your pious . . . habit of regarding the world as a moral gymnasium built expressly to strengthen your character in occasionally leads you to think about your own confounded principles when you should be thinking about other people's necessities."

Before the important 1944 presidential election a prominent Christian writer said he would vote for the Prohibition Party.

Why? The reason he gave was that they didn't bombard him with propaganda. He, like others, seemed to think that the election was sort of a demure registration of preferences; the idea seemed to be, to express oneself quietly, without getting stained by association with the crowd, on the side of the purest candidate, and then to leave the whole nasty business. The smaller the group one supports, the less their power, the less likelihood of actual victory (and, of course, the nicer the people), the better.

" He's so *sincere* "

Or the motives with which the moral man is concerned may be those of the leader. The cliché, " I vote for the man," is often uttered with a note of self-congratulation, as though this made the speaker morally better than partisan folk. The implication is that politics is a sort of popularity or character contest, in which the substance of positions can be ignored.

American Protestantism often has assumed that one need only be concerned with the good intentions of individuals, and can leave aside considerations of policy, program, and interest. It's a handy idea — but it's wrong.

"Sincerity" is not the only question, even about the individual. Remember Johnny, the boy next door? He was a very *sincere* trumpet player!

Usually, there are good, sincere men on both sides; the political question is not their " goodness " or " sincerity," but the groups and policies they represent.

Also, when one candidate appears " good " to churchfolk, another not so good, it is often observable that the " good " one is very much like the churchfolk themselves in class, habit, manner, national origin, and style, whereas the dubious one comes from another background. Hiding under many references to " integrity," " sincerity," " character," " independence," " dignity " in politics is the unspoken awareness: He's like us; he's our kind.

The unawareness of power

The advantage of the lifeboat or desert island is that it removes the larger problems of power. The attitude of many religious folk is to pretend those problems don't exist. They know the quotation from Lord Acton about absolute power corrupting absolutely, but they don't know that it only tells part of the story, and doesn't tell that very well. It is the *love* of power, the anxious, egotistical seeking and glorying in power, that corrupts; since men are such that, almost inevitably, power brings out such egotism, Action was almost right in saying that power itself corrupts. But *lack of power also corrupts;* rather, the same egotism (or, if you will, sinfulness) is at work in *the shunning of power* (the avoiding of the energy and discipline and responsibility of power, the pretending to be pure, stainless, better as a result). Worse, still, is the unwillingness to acknowledge, or to use responsibly, the power one has.

On not having to meet a payroll

The moralistic errors we have described appear in all kinds of politics; the conservative's version is like that we noted above, with morality joining religion in embracing the interests of those who want to preserve the prevailing order. But let's talk, as we promised earlier in this chapter, about the other " progressive " or " reformer " side.

Here the fault often is idealism. The idealist begins with an abstract list of good things, drawn out of the mind — equality, peace, justice — instead of with the world as it is. He misses the fact that politics is not just about pure ideals, but about *policy* — that is, about relating particular objectives to other objectives and to what's possible; especially, he ignores the facts about power and interest and responsibility.

Much Protestant idealism, though not pacifist, is pacifistic, very much inclined to see all that is military as bad in itself, a position that leads outside the actual political contest, because the policies really contending for power are going to have a military element. Though strong for " peace," this position may be against the means to work for peace, through alliance systems like NATO. The idealist's preference would be to do things through the UN. The UN, once underestimated, may now, by such attitudes, be overestimated. Why? Because it's not what the idealist wants to think it is — a governing body of some kind. It has no real power, except that which its members give it; the votes of its general assembly do not relieve a powerful member like the United States from responsibly making up its own mind what its interests and commitments require. Also, there is no automatic virtue in positions arrived at by the vote of many nations.

The progressive's form of morality, beginning with a blueprint for an ideal world, often fails to notice that it does not fit the possibilities of this one. His humanitarian programs often assume that men are rational and filled with good will, and that they will moderate their desires to fit in with what is just. The progressive, or " liberal," as we call him, has a list of " good " groups, like the labor unions, Negroes, Jews, the poor, the immigrants, the emerging anticolonial nations, toward whom he is rather uncritically enthusiastic. He tends to oversimplify problems like those of colonialism, in an unwillingness to grant the mixtures of goods and evils and the problems of change. He has a list of " good " causes and issues, also rather stereotyped and oversimplified, in which his human sympathies can find expression. Where his opposite number, the moralistic conservative, characteristically lacks a sharp sense of justice, the moralistic liberal has that sense in the extreme, but lacks a political wisdom to go with it. Of course one can *imagine* better arrangements, in an ideal world; but in this world we must see first where we are. We must count the cost and know the limits of change; we must recognize that change brings new problems with it; and we must know that our own solutions are partial. We keep doing the best we can with what we've got.

All political issues are and yet are not " moral " issues

The whole idea of the " moral issue " is dangerous because it tends to lead toward a small, select, rather stereotyped and often even trivial set of problems.

It implies that " bingo " is a moral issue — and public housing is not; that " liquor " is a moral issue — but Federal aid to education is not; that grain for India is a moral issue — but the depletion allowance on oil is not; that economic aid abroad is " moral " — but military aid is not. All political issues are, in a sense, moral issues; it is not helpful to select items for emphasis on the basis of which can be called " moral "; often that leads away from the more difficult and important problems to the edges and corners.

Identifying problems as moral issues also may have the ironic result of relieving, rather than increasing, moral tension. Suppose we are told that the racial problem is really a *moral* issue in the heart of the white man. That is true. Still, putting it so may relieve us rather than pull us toward constructive action. We may say that all that is required is a change in attitude — in moral intention on the part of the white man — and since of course I have no prejudice, therefore I have done my part. I, therefore, need not further investigate the *structure* of prejudice, built into the society of which I am a participating member; I need not organize and participate in the politics that might alter those structures. No, the problem is a *moral* one. The church has drained off much energy in this way, focusing its members too much on their own motives and attitudes, too little on what exists outside and needs to be done.

The heart of this moralistic error, in all its forms, is this: it turns away from the world to look instead at what " my position " is. It asks not, " What justice can we help the world to yield? " but rather, " Am I right? Is my position pure? " The focus is altogether too much on motives, on abstract principles, on a moral realm of the imagination, altogether too little on facts, conditions, powers, possibilities. In a way, despite its elevated ethical language, this position is too self-centered: it looks, if we may recall Bernard Shaw again, at the self's " confounded principles " instead of " other people's necessities." In another way, it is too easy. It offers a way around the infinite and continuing difficulties, intellectual, moral, and practical, of the political world. Monetary policy, and military strategy in a nuclear world, are hard to understand — but a good man's motives are easy. The organization of the combination of interests to make a net advance on civil rights or Federal aid to education is hard — but a " moral crusade " is easy. Everyone can be for that.

Nothing here is to be taken as being against morality or religion; of course not. That's no platform to run on. But the problem is not just endorsing them; the problem is applying them to particular cases. And that means more talk about the details of the case, less about morality and religion. It is more important that we *be* moral than that we keep labeling ourselves as such. And to *be* moral, in a political situation, requires political understanding.

Religion may or may not be a good thing for American democracy. It depends.

CHAPTER

4

CHRISTIANITY'S CONTRIBUTION TO POLITICS

So far we have approached our subject mainly from the side of politics. But what does Christian faith really have to do with all this very worldly world?

In one sense, the answer is: not much. One of the most important things to say about faith and politics is that faith does not have, *first of all,* much to do with politics.

It does not deal primarily with levels of taxation or price supports for corn or policy toward China or local school bond issues or segregation in street cars or the control of Suez or atom bomb tests or the size of the budget.

Neither is Christian faith most essentially about " moral and spiritual values " or " principles " for politics or " ideals " for society, or even the " religious experience " or " spiritual values " or " yearning for a higher power " to which political questions may be vaguely related.

A Drama Acted on a Big Stage

What is Christian faith about, first of all? It is an old, strange, incredible story about what God has done for man's salvation, and there are eleven other books in this Layman's series which tell different parts of the story.

This story, which is the heart of Christian faith, goes *far* beyond politics, and does not yield *any* direct and unequivocal answers to political questions.

(But that is itself a contribution to politics!)

The story talks about the " soul " of man — something of him that goes deeper than the politics of earth can reach; it points to a beginning and an end of life that go beyond what politics can control; it insists that there is more here than that which is to be rendered to Caesar.

What political contribution can be found in a faith that points beyond politics? For a starter, just that: " politics " — the human choosing and wanting and doing — is not the whole story.

At least that means an opposition (as the rhetoric of the campaign speech goes, an " unalterable " opposition) to the totalitarianism that reaches out a political hand to try to grasp the very soul of man. Even the, seemingly, most irrelevant of faiths and churches may suddenly turn out to have a great earthly significance, as churches did in Nazi Germany, when the issue is put as sharply as a totalitarian state can put it.

But what about the times and places in which the issue is *not* put that sharply? Has Christianity nothing to say then? It ought then also to bring the same message it brings in times of great trial — the message that the political drama is played out on a stage that's larger than its own intentions perceive. A big stage. That makes a difference.

The God this story tells about stands above the politics of every age. He ruled the earth through all those tedious ages when Formosa and Cyprus and trouble spots generally were gradually breaking off from the mainland or rising up from the sea, or doing whatever thing they did to come into being. He made the soil in which crops, both basic and nonbasic, have always grown, in which, season after season, throughout all ages, " first the seed and then the ear and the full corn will appear," and now the surplus of full corn will appear. He "created out of nothing" the vast stretches of Nevada desert and the Pacific atolls, which man's ingenuity in discovering and his ineptitude in employing nuclear fission now threaten to return to nothing.

When Christians speak of his "justice" they mean a justice that transcends and judges the world's imperfect justice; when they speak of his "righteousness" they mean a righteousness that stands over against the acts of courts, jails, investigating committees, mediation boards, and pressure groups. His "love" stands in contrast to the calculations of self-interest, "enlightened" or otherwise, in terms of which political warfare is fought. He asks a devotion radically different from the expedient, shifting, partisan devotions of politics. He offers a hope quite beyond the fragile human hopes for guaranteed annual wages, "a full dinner pail," a classless society, or "peace in our time."

But doesn't all this "beyond" and "above" and "before" business, all this that's "more" than meets the eye, all this that the theologician calls "transcendence" — doesn't all this amount to the religionism that retreats to a separate and otherworldly domain, that we condemned in the last chapter?

Wrongly understood, yes. Rightly understood, no.

The Two Parts of the Christian Story

We note two parts in the Christian story: (1) the "transcendence" we mentioned, but also, (2) the remarkable relation of the God who is transcendent to the life of man. Let's look at these in turn.

1. *Men Are Not Gods.* The political meaning of the first point (transcendence) is this: it strikes down any human claim

of absoluteness, finality, completeness; therefore it insists always on a degree of openness, a tentativeness, a sitting loose in the saddle; it leaves room for the mystery and unexpectedness of life, and for the other fellow's opinion. People like the communists, or the social engineers — or, for that matter, any of us — who think we've got human life bottled up in our own little scheme, who think we are master of our own destiny (let alone anybody else's), find out differently.

It is important for Christians to realize that this applies to their own " Christian " programs quite as much as to others. The point has been made — perhaps overmade — that no political achievement is to be identified with Christianity or the will of God. It is a commonplace of contemporary religious writing to say that there is no " Christian system," or no " Christian way " in politics and economics, and society. But let's say it again: There is *no* arrangement of society that is to be identified with God, or the Bible, or Jesus' teaching, or Christianity, or religion: not capitalism or socialism; not conservatism or liberalism; not any Republican or Democratic platform or the pro or the con of any political issue; certainly not communism, but not anticommunism, as a political movement, either; not *any* of the decisions, policies, programs, projects, and causes that we arrange.

2. *God's Love Is the Center*. But if that first point is clear, then there's the second: the story tells more about God than that he is transcendent, beyond, away up there, eternal. It also, and this is the incredible part, claims to tell what he does and something of what he's like. Reasonable people from the Greeks on up have found this hard. Maybe they can get the part about transcendence, about an original, powerful Being, beyond the world and yet in charge of it. But then to say that that God — the ultimate One behind it all — was somehow in one particular man (Jesus) at one particular time

(when Pontius Pilate was procurator of Judaea), that he "suffered" and all the rest of it — well, that's not really very logical. For the Christian, nevertheless, that's the important part of the story: it answers, as no logic could, as no idea out of his own head could, the most important questions in the world. It says that the ultimate power is in some sense "personal." (It makes a big difference in politics, and life generally, whether you look on the universe as an impersonal machine or not.) The story means that man, inextricably tangled in himself, is always being offered a way ahead — not by his own power, exactly, but not by magic, either — rather, by accepting the "love," the "forgiveness" that's extended to him from God. Words like "love" and "forgiveness" have to be added to the other word, transcendence, before we begin to get the force of it.

The language of Christianity, so powerful in its own place, gets spoiled by easy overuse, and has the meaning drained by familiarity and glibness. This book has tried hard to make clear that the ultimate matters of Christian faith are a long, long, *long* way from the give-and-take of the day's politics. But, nevertheless, the heart of Christianity's relation to politics is in its central idea: God in Christ, reconciling the world to himself; God's offered love, man's love to neighbor in response.

But don't talk about it too much in the legislature or ward meeting.

This Has Indirect, but Important, Meaning in Politics

So now back to politics. How does all this (especially the part about God's being "love" and "forgiveness") relate to day-to-day life? Certainly, in one sense, very indirectly. In fact, if we think about what goes on in the used-car market or the domestic relations court or the board of trade or the House

Rules Committee or even in our own office, we may be tempted to say that "indirectly" is hardly the word for it!

Christianity gives no precise answer to any of the dilemmas of life — certainly not the political ones. But it provides what's more important: direction, understanding, commitment. There is no "Christian" position — but there *are* better and worse positions, relatively just and relatively unjust acts, and the Christian should seek what is good and just. Moreover, this story helps to illuminate what is "just" and how we have failed to accord with it.

The relation between Christian faith and politics is indirect, but it can be very important.

It is indirect, not in the sense that it deals with individuals rather than with social structures; not in the sense that it deals with moral rather than political issues; it is indirect in that it intends to bring a dimension of commitment and understanding, rather than the precise details of a position.

In the next chapter we will discuss the kind of *guide* for politics that Christianity can furnish, and in the chapters after that, the sort of *understanding* of politics it can bring.

5

LOVE AND JUSTICE

If we ask what guidance the Christian story can give to political action, the answer would probably contain the word "love." There aren't any final principles or laws, we would be told; there is only a relationship, indicated by that word. The most important guideline is summarized in the great commandment about loving God and neighbor.

Unfortunately, like many other religious words, the word "love" is almost spoiled by misuse and confusion of meaning. It has become terribly sentimental, connoting some gush of feeling, and some hopelessly ideal condition. Moreover, it is almost exclusively confined to individual relations.

And the sentimental, individualistic, and ideal versions of the word "love" won't be much help with the problems we are talking about here.

But those versions don't really reflect all that the word means. Let's take the hardest use of all and stay with it for a while: "Love your enemies."

Here, at least, there is a helpfully realistic note; the phrase assumes that one will have enemies. It does not say, "Love people, and you will have no enemies." The Bible treats men as real creatures in time and place, with real commitments, real interests, real opponents.

Love and Conflict

Too many churchfolk assume that the teaching about "love" means they should ignore political struggles. But the pretense that there is no conflict here — that there is a simple harmony among men of good will — is contrary to fact and to the Bible's claims.

Sometimes Christians are shocked to see that there is conflict "even" in a Christian community. A student at a youth conference, shaken after the first day of floor debate, came to the chairman to say that he'd never believed Christians could fight with one another that way! But they can, as any battle-scarred veteran of church meetings knows. In certain contexts, they should. In a sense it is our duty to our enemy to oppose him. It is our obligation to defend what we see to be true and valuable.

The proponents of harmony and tolerance, so numerous in the Protestant community, may not be serving the larger value after all. They may be sacrificing truth to harmony, encouraging a sleepy acquiescence in whatever happens. They may, in fact, be serving the interest of those who have what they want and don't want to see the boat rocked.

"Love" does not mean that we refrain from opposing and resisting our opponents. We need to know what, and who, should be opposed. Don't try to deny that conflict exists. Admit it. Then try to make it serve useful purposes.

But does love have any meaning if the fight continues? Yes, it does. It means that in all our struggling there is never a *final* enmity. The struggling and conflict take place within a larger framework of affirmation and unity.

Here is an analogy: G. K. Chesterton wrote that "tolerance is the virtue of people who don't believe anything." Perhaps, in this overtolerant age, we can amend that to say that toler-

ance is *only* a virtue in those who *do* believe something. It is
easy for moderns who have little if any interest in problems of
religious *truth* to be very tolerant of religious differences; it is
not so easy for a man who *really believes* in the distinction
between true and false, and for whom religion is a central and
not a minor part of life. But his is the real tolerance; it is the
result, not of a shrug of the shoulders, but of his conviction of
the truth — a truth that he knows transcends his stating of it.

Similarly, " love " is not noteworthy within the circle of one's
own friends and supporters. (" Do not even the publicans the
same? ") It has force and meaning in the midst of conviction,
conflict, and opposition.

The Necessity and the Limit of Opposition

Americans can learn something here from their much-
disdained politicians. From the galleries the citizens are startled to see two legislators, recently in fiery debate against each
other, now walk off arm in arm in quiet and friendly conver-
sation. The citizens are startled because they haven't sufficiently
learned to understand the democratic political discipline: to
care deeply about issues that one nevertheless must submit to
the give-and-take of politics; to oppose a man forcefully today,
knowing still that he may be an ally tomorrow; to honor a
friend but still to investigate for oneself and often to disagree
with him; to oppose people at one level while maintaining
unity with them at another.

Too often we tend rather to pretend everyone is true blue,
to take all claims at face value, to assume harmonious agreement, to discourage the intellectual energy and political alert-
ness that discerns *issues* and fights over them; and, then, when
some disagreement *does* force its way to the front to make the
disagreement ultimate — one side " right," the other " wrong ";

to take opposition (being unused to it) very personally, as an affront, and to make it absolute; to leave no room for levels of agreement and disagreement, for differences of opinion and interest and intellectual conviction.

McCarthyism was the hard, extreme version of this: relative matters of opinion were turned into absolute matters of loyalty. There was no allowance for simple disagreement on Far Eastern policy; those who differed had to be looked at as "traitors," and a "party of treason."

Much of the religious community in a very different way, falls into a soft version of the same error; and the inability to talk about politics rationally is a sign of it. Disagreement, opposition, conflict: these are taken emotionally, as contradictory to the Christian spirit; and so problems are glossed over and left unexamined, because there does not exist the ability to "speak the truth in love," to disagree while yet affirming each other.

But Christian faith does have the resources for the democratic political discipline, right in its most central teachings. Although the legislators on Capitol Hill and in the Statehouse would be aghast to hear it so described, it is nevertheless true in a sense, as a Christian historian has written, that parliamentary democracy is founded on the "forgiveness of sins." We reunite today with those whom we opposed yesterday; our breakings and unitings are surrounded by vast areas of common affirmation — and, more, by unbroken personal acceptance of each other. And so, in the parts of life from which at first glance the claim of love seems most remote, it may in the end be most relevant.

In the midst of the political wars Christians can help to keep an awareness that differences, though sharp and important, are not ultimate — and that the area of agreement in America is enormously larger than the area of disagreement.

The differences among Americans over Federal aid to education and recognition of Communist China and segregation and
corporation taxes are less basic than an agreement on the means
for solving these disputes. We are basically agreed upon the
right of the majority to rule, and the right of the minority
to civil liberties and the ground rules of freedom, and this
agreement is more important than any immediate disagreement.

Conflict, Love, and Communist Enemies

But there's more to it than that. Even where there is no such
area of common agreement, the injunction to love and forgive
still applies. No man has the right to speak the word of final
rejection and denial of another. This applies even to the most
extreme enemies. Today, this means the communists.

The communists are fundamentally opposed to us and to
what we stand for. We should not obscure that fact. The communist system resolutely denies the grandeur of man, in a
brutal collectivist system with spies on spies, brain-washing,
slave-labor camps, and a terrifying nonchalance about the life
and freedom of man. Communism employs a utopian vision
of a justice that will come tomorrow to justify the cruelest
activities today. Therefore, the brutal acts of the communist
system are not, so to speak, the personal cruelty of a perverted
man, but the cold, impersonal scientific brutality of a fanatical
system confident it is serving an ultimately higher end.

Against such a group, what can forgiveness of sins mean?
It means that, however thoroughgoing opposition to the communist may be, there is never the final denial of his humanity.
The rule still must be, as it is in our domestic differences, oppose and forgive.

The Christian cannot join these extreme anticommunists
who describe communists as " rats." The psychology of such

an identification is clear: having identified the enemy with a pest, one can "exterminate" him without feelings of pity or human responsibility. Such a mentality is frightening, not only in what it does to the victims, but also in what it does to the hunters. We deny our own humanity when we regard fellow human beings as less than human.

Christians not only should love the heretic, while hating the heresy; they also should remain open to the partial truth and to the judgment upon themselves a "heresy" may contain, and to the many varieties of human living and thinking and desiring it may reflect. We are inclined to think in too wooden a fashion about "the communists" and "the Russians." To be a "communist" may mean something quite different in Russia, Yugoslavia, Malaya, China, France, the U.S.A.; in 1917, 1933, 1957; in different individuals in the same time and place. Americans who visit Russia, or read some communist novels, awake with a start to the realization that the daily muddles and meanings of ordinary human life go on even in these "enemy" lands.

This does not mean that the political contest can be ignored or done away with by appeals to the "people" of communist lands. It does not mean that, because we accept the judgment that communism represents on our defects we therefore believe those defects are anywhere nearly as bad as the fundamental evils in communism. It does not mean that, because some individuals become communists for relatively good reasons that the communist movement is to be opposed any less forcefully. It does not mean that, because we are all human, our political conflict can be easily resolved or forgotten or prosecuted with any less vigor. But it does mean that we should never allow our political and military contests to wipe from our hearts the fellow feeling with the common human base upon which these tragedies of history are built.

Against Making Stereotypes and Villains

In a world that is complicated, specialized, and impersonal, we seek villains and heroes, partly because as participants in causing evil we need a way to excuse ourselves, and partly because as victims of evildoing we insist upon finding a personal culprit responsible for our distress.

As we feel the bite of higher prices on our limited supply of money, we get mad at the grocer, or the farmers, or labor unions, or at the " bloodsucking profiteers," or at the " rascals " in Washington who aren't doing enough, or are doing too much, or anyway, something. We cannot unload this burden on a complex and essentially impersonal economic explanation of the high prices. When we are told that such an explanation might demand much higher taxes, we get even angrier, and denounce bureaucrats still more fervently. Like the Okie in *Grapes of Wrath,* who was shoved off his land, we want to know what *man* is responsible, and we are baffled when we are told that the man before us just works for a company that is owned by a bank. We cannot get mad at a graph. These emotional forces, seeking a personal symbol to blame, far outrun our rational ability to understand a system and locate its defects.

This drive toward dramatic and emotional oversimplification is not confined to extreme movements. There is at least a touch of it in the symbols of most political thinking: in the Republican's attack on " labor bosses," " liberals " (or " so-called liberals "), " eggheads," " city machines "; in the Democrat's attack on " special interests " and " big business." Underneath the legitimate simplification there may be an illegitimate stereotype.

Against Vindictiveness

Our enemies evoke not only a righteous but also an extra, unrighteous indignation. This tendency in us is increased when the enemy is a group rather than an individual, and we talk about the communist, Jap, Hun, capitalist, radical, subversive, or nigger-lover. In wartime, the enemy is pictured in a brutal image, and vindictive themes run through the plans for victory.

A role of the Christian in such situations may be illuminated by the position of some Christians in the events surrounding World War II. A few Christian leaders tried to counteract the pacifist and isolationist sentiment within the American Protestant community in the late thirties. They directed attention to the evil that Hitler and the Nazi movement in Germany represented. They joined in this enterprise with a great many other political figures from the general American society. But after we were embarked upon the war against Germany some of these same Protestant leaders opposed measures like the "Morgenthau Plan" to reduce Germany to the level of an agricultural economy. Anxious to have America enter the war to oppose Germany, they were, nevertheless, anxious to avoid a vindictive treatment of Germany in defeat.

For the Unlovely

But Christianity goes farther than the humane counsel against villain-making and vindictiveness (a counsel that civilized men generally accept). It goes on to insist that the affirmation of the neighbor should not depend upon his virtue or innocence. It marks the decisive break with the tribal morality that loves only those who are the innocent and virtuous members of the group; it teaches instead a love for the unlovely, the outcast, the guilty. It does not, therefore, necessitate falling into the sentimental assumption that those whom we love are guiltless, good people who " merit " our love.

Goodhearted people sometimes have a tendency to idealize those whose rights they wish to protect. For example, a group of ministers were agitated because a Negro, apparently largely because he was a Negro, was charged with a crime that he did not, in fact, commit. Their campaign for justice for him, however, was somewhat upset when they discovered that the man, although innocent of the particular crime, was guilty of many other crimes and was, on the whole, a rascal. They would have preferred to have sought justice for a Negro who was a " good " man! Again, the churchfolk are startled to discover that the refugee they've helped to come to this country is not a romantic hero of freedom, and is definitely not interested in coming to their church. Actually, the problem of justice is always obtaining justice for " bad " people — that is, for people who don't fit our expectations. And love goes beyond justice to mercy and forgiveness for " bad " people.

The Distinctive Note in Christian Love

Perhaps our preachments too often imply that Christians are unique in seeking to love the neighbor who is everyman, an implication that the lives of many worthy members of other religions and of no religion refute every day. However, the way the Christian understands this link to the neighbor is different: the link is not just the common humanity of men bound in the bundle of life. Beyond that there is the link implied in the Christian story itself.

That means that the love does not begin with the man himself. The center of it, rather, is in the love of God; the point about this fellow is not that he's a good man, or that we're in the same boat, but that God's forgiveness extends, alike, to him and to me.

Love, in its use in the New Testament, has an overflowing, extra quality, pre-eminently in God's love for man, but also then in the love a man extends to his neighbor. It is not just a love for that which is lovable, but extends beyond to seek out the lost sheep. It is a love not grounded in the deserts and merits of the beloved one, but overflowing from the nature of the lover. God so loves the world because it is his nature to love, not because the world deserves it; he comes across the gap on his own initiative, so to speak, to meet man, to offer him a " reconciliation." He does what man did not deserve, or merit, or earn. The love of neighbor reflects this divine initiative; man may be able to love his neighbor because his own condition has been taken care of by the forgiveness God has offered.

Love's Representative: Justice

But, having said all this, we must now go on to another major point: " love " is not enough — at least, not as it is sometimes understood, for it may mean that the charity basket approach has been used instead of the attempt by political and economic reform to change the social conditions that make the charity basket necessary. Often the argument against social change is based on the loving-kindness of individual exceptions to a system that is wrong — for example, the gentle slaveowner who " loved his slaves," and who told them to " love " him in return.

Therefore, in social affairs, love must be represented, so to speak, by the " justice " or " righteousness " that the prophets spoke about.

Justice implies some kind of merit, of worth, of desert, of what is " due "; justice means what's coming to me. Where love in its fullest Christian sense ignores, dwarfs, and overcomes all question of merit in a forgiving love of the unlovely, justice, on the contrary, *emphasizes* that merit and desert. And in political ethics that emphasis is necessary. Why? An illustration:

People in the shacks of the company town tear up and destroy the gift baskets of food that are sent them from well-meaning wives of owners of the company, in their rather larger houses on the other side of town. They say, " We want not charity, but *justice.*" This is the cry of social reform: not gifts, not something that is given out of the largess of the owner (and therefore tainted with condescension); rather they demand what they *deserve,* what is due, what is *just.*

Love of the unlovely is offensive if it includes an implication that the lover knows the lovee *is* unlovely, but loves him anyway; forgiveness is an insult if the recipient was unaware of any need to be forgiven.

The ultimate Christian story has meaning only when it begins with penitence, humility, and contrition on the part of the believer; otherwise, the cocky answer to God's gracious gift is "No, thanks." Always, in relation to God, that's the wrong answer; sometimes, in relation to a neighbor, it's the right one.

A great deal of the trouble that Christianity has caused in politics is the result of having its personal truth misplaced. At the very last point Christian faith ignores social facts and addresses itself to a man in his solitariness, but that does not mean that Christianity is unaware of social nature of the self. The Christian teaching about the uniqueness and value of every individual soul in the eyes of God is an ultimate truth; but it can make trouble if it is applied too immediately, so that one overlooks the power of society in shaping the individual, and the importance of society to the life of the individual.

Love and Justice Need Each Other

So "love" by itself is not enough; but neither, then, is "justice." No system of social reform, no change in social and economic conditions, no good society, no "new America" will enable us to dispense with ordinary individual kindness and helpfulness. Lots of times the love of the neighbor in the ghetto and in Japan and in Hungary does not have its counterpart in the love of neighbor in the apartment upstairs. The nasty wrangling and unpleasant dealing with one another among people devoted to good causes is always a fit subject for ironic comment. Nevertheless, one must avoid the temptation of a certain kind of pious Christian therefore to conclude that the organizational and reforming activities are distinctly secondary in importance. The saintly figure who remains impervious to the struggles for justice, and simply deals as nicely as he can with the individuals he meets, may be more to be criticized than the passionate social reformer who forgets to pay his own secretary a living wage and barks nastily at her in his attempt to get something done.

Like most of the key words that come out of the Bible to shape the Christian view — words like "faith" and "love" — the word "justice" in its Biblical and Christian sense has an active and personal quality. Therefore, when we think of justice as that Greek goddess, blindfolded, with the scales, we do not have quite the right image of "justice" in this sense. The "justice" the Christian talks about is more than that of the law court, of the heritage of Roman law, of equal measure and balanced judgment, of appropriate rewards and punishments — important though all those are. Justice in the Bible's sense includes all of this, but there is more.

And that's where love comes in again. For as love is not fully love unless it expresses itself in justice, so justice is always being redefined upward in the light of Christian love. In a sense, when you ask ultimately what men deserve in the eyes of the justice of the Bible, they " deserve " more than they deserve. Men have more coming to them than any worthfulness in them would merit, because the Christian view of the whole show is arranged, not on a neat balance of rewards and punishment, but rather on a new basis in which God forgives and offers his gracious power to every sinner. Therefore, at the last, the measures of merit and right in worldly terms are done away; love defines Christian justice, and they come together. But, meanwhile, don't overlook the justice part.

Something Wrong with the System

A sense of justice requires an awareness of social arrangements. One must recognize that there can be *structural* faults in the society, apart from the villainy or goodness of particular individuals. Good and evil lodge in the pattern of social relations, affecting mightily the individuals who live within it.

This is not to take the mistaken and unchristian view that good and evil are wholly the result of impersonal social forces, so that if we just rearrange the environment with the right kind of social engineering, then everything will be all right.

But neither is it to take the opposite and equally mistaken view (to which Christians are much more tempted) that good and evil are wholly the result of the free decision of untrammeled individual wills, so that if each of us will please right now just stand up straight and, by golly, decide to be decent, then everything will be all right.

This last view is correct in seeing that the source of moral evil is the heart of man, and not any social system; but it is wrong in believing that the will of an individual is free from the influence of others and of the habits of his society. Part of what original sin means is that we are preceded by a wrong decision already taken. Things were "loused up" before we got here. And yet, in a way, we are responsible for the situation, because the wrongness is not just out there, in the way things go in the world, but also in us, in the way we respond to it and make it worse.

And the evil that springs from the heart of man leaves a deposit in the systems of society — not only in the obviously cruel and unjust institutions, but in all of them. Even a social arrangement that we might all endorse, like, say, democracy, has its own peculiar difficulties and dangers, as we shall see in a later chapter.

Segregation Is a Structure of Injustice

Racial segregation is an example of what we have been saying; it is a pattern, a bad habit, of society that works its own evil.

It hurts those who are its victims — but it is also harmful to those who maintain it and to the whole society.

It has affected the Negro, not only by denying him the better school, or the front seat of the bus, or admission to the hospital, but also, more importantly, in his status and self-estimation.

The outward effects of segregation can be read in many indexes — for example, in those of the mortality of Negro children or the markedly lower life expectancy of Negroes than whites. The inner effects are even more important, not only in what they do to the Negro, but in what they do to the white man: they can be seen in the self-abasement of the one, and the self-deception of the other. The line in the society and the line in the mind reinforce each other: prejudice makes segregation and segregation makes prejudice, in a circle of evil.

Racial segregation illustrates the way a structure of injustice works, because it creates its own seeming justification: the segregation of Negroes for several generations has created the lower educational and cultural conditions that are now cited by segregationists to "prove" their point and oppose integrated schools. Years of enforced inferiority create indexes of crime and delinquency that are used as "proof" that the Negro is inferior. Thus there is a kind of self-reinforcing evil in the system itself.

This structure illustrates the point, too, that social injustice may be defended by persons who are "good" and "Christian." It is surely a mistake to assume that racial segregation is defended only by those who fit neatly into the stereotype of the demagogue. Such built-in social arrangements affect, and are defended by, large segments of whole regions (and, elsewhere, nations) including, of course, many "good" men.

The church will play an important part in the long unraveling of the last threads of the segregation system, and to play that part it will need all the wisdom it can muster. The church will need to be clear about the injustice of segregation, without making it the only absolute evil; it will need to have sympathy for the problems of the white community of the Deep South (so very different from anything Northerners know about) without overlooking the more fundamental problems of the Negro community and without faltering in the national insistence that the segregation *system* is wrong and must go.

The point may be illustrated by reference to the commonly heard remarks against the "two extremes" (e.g., the NAACP and the White Citizens' Councils) in the civil rights struggle. The use of this phrase obscures the important fact that one "extreme," whatever its strategic and other errors, has a fundamental relation to justice that the other, whatever its partial truths, does not.

Dealing with a complicated problem like this requires not

only a clear sense of justice but at the same time self-criticism, historical wisdom, and love. One hates the evil of segregation, to be sure; but one should not overlook the fact that it is easier for a white man to come to that moral stand when he is safely separated from the problem in some Northern retreat. We should not expect to see the system removed overnight, or expect all racial problems to be ended in that happy day when segregation is no more. Though the problem at bottom is one of justice, there is still no room here for self-righteousness, and there is plenty of room for compassion.

MAN'S SELF-INTEREST AND HIS CONSCIENCE

The "transcendence" and "forgiveness" of which Christians speak are intended to say something not only of God but also (at the same time) about the way we think of ourselves and of our continuing enterprise, human history. In this chapter we will look at a Christian view of man, and in the next a Christian view of history, as they apply to our thinking about politics.

Sin and Self-interest

The much discussed doctrine of "sin" doesn't mean just ordinary wrongdoing; it means that basic and inextricable tangle of the self in itself that becomes fully visible only as the rest of the Christian story — especially about God's forgiveness — is brought in. But this sin — this tangle of the self — has generally visible results, and has these not only in the individual but also in the relations of groups. The example that it is most important to understand in politics is the way everyone is affected by the interests and biases of the groups of which he is a part.

Begin with something like a church volleyball game at the Y.M.C.A. There are the men from First Church playing the men from Trinity: good Christian men all of them. But when the ball lands near the line an interesting configuration appears: all the good Christian men on one side agree that the ball was out, while all the good Christian men on the other side say that it was in.

Of course, when the older boys puff around on the court just for the fun of it, there are not many such arguments; then each side can often agree that it lost the point. But, suppose the game is for the championship. That's harder. And then, suppose it's not a game, but for keeps — for houses, cars, and vacations for the family; for power, for status and self-respect. Then we are no longer making a joke; then it's serious. And then we begin to know the force of "interests" on the mind.

By "interests" we mean all that is self-protecting and self-advancing, everything in which "I" have a stake as over against "you." These interests are not simply economic, though economic ones are basic and cannot be overlooked. There are many other kinds: the ego's stake in its power, in protecting itself and gaining victories, especially in saving face, in receiving deference, in gaining prestige.

The fact of group interest appears plainly in organized form: when the petroleum industry wants the states to control the Tidelands or the National Association of Real Estate Boards opposes public housing. But there is something much more important than these obvious forms: the effect of group interest upon the mind of everyone.

Interests not only color men's judgments about what concrete acts are good; they color also the very definition of the good. We hear and notice things selectively: sister's hearing is bad when the dishes are to be done, but improves remarkably when the postman starts up the walk. Each of us has built into his mind not only his own selective self-protection, but that of his groups: years of interested interpretation on behalf of the South, of the American middle class, of farmers, of business, of the old Yankee stock, of race, class, and nation.

The men on the volleyball court on one side probably really do think the ball was in; those on the other side really think it was out. When a fender is dented, each driver really does think that the other was at fault. Men in upper-income brackets really do regard our progressive income tax rate as " confiscatory " and unjust; men in lower-income brackets really do regard it as just.

Though there are always many, many individual exceptions, the preponderant attitudes of particular groups and classes are rather easily predictable. Using party affiliation as a handy indication of a number of other things, one can predict, for example, that if a man is a small-town, old-stock, upper-income Protestant businessman, he is likely to be a Republican; if he is a big-city, lower-income immigrant Catholic workingman, a Democrat. Or, if your city is in the North, whatever it is, we may predict that the " better " residential areas are Republican, the inner-city, industrial, and tenement areas Democratic.

One may protest that all we are saying is the obvious thing, that a man's attitudes reflect his background and his identifications. That's right. But what may be overlooked in that obvious statement is: (1) how *deeply* his background does affect his thinking, and (2) how subtly and universally the *interests* of groups affect that background.

Different Groups Think Differently

Inequalities among men are more inevitable and more necessary than we like to admit. There are obvious natural and developed differences among men, in strength, in energy, in brains, in leadership, in character, in dexterity, in many things, and these differences are often large and important. The working of society requires that these inequalities be used: left-handed people to do left-handed things, brainy people to do brainy things, strong people to lift pianos. It also requires that additional distinctions be developed to lead, to create, to preserve culture, to think, to build, to get businessmen to take risks, to get the sand hogs to dig the Lincoln Tunnel, to fill all the society's diverse and necessary functions. But around these necessary natural and developed inequalities there grow *un*necessary further distinctions of prestige, deference, power, and emolument, and with these grow different ways of thinking that include an element of rationalization of the group's position. Those who profit from the inequalities tend to find them justifiable; those who are left out tend to find them unjustifiable. When one is young and poor, the wealth and status of the aged and privileged look like the result of luck, and pull, and maybe a little cheating; as one gets older and richer those advantages more and more appear to have been *earned*. To so-called "underdeveloped" nations, America's vast wealth and power often appear illegitimate and annoying; to us, they usually seem the result of virtue, right thinking, and hard work. There is usually some measure of truth on each side, since each seizes upon whatever congenial truths it can find.

Morality as Self-defense

The pull of interest on thought means that moral ideas cannot be taken at face value. Moral claims have a tendency to turn into defensiveness and self-justification.

We know what ordinary, everyday defensiveness is like. It is plain in the child: "I didn't do it, Johnny did it. I have been good all day." So he justifies himself — adults do it a little more subtly — and claims what is good for himself and imputes what is evil to others. This defensiveness is more subtle when men justify themselves, not just by claiming all good, but by defining the understanding of good in such a way that they come out higher than others. Each of us may tend to regard as good and right that in which we come off best. No statement of a moral or political position can be taken as final, not because there is no final moral claim, but because all statements of it may be used in self-defense.

For example: " Freedom " can be the battle cry of those who fight tyranny, or the slogan of those who increase profits; " individual dignity " may be the source of respect for an employee, or the excuse for breaking his union. The ideal of equality may be used to criticize the unjustified, unequal advantages that accrue to me, or simply and solely to challenge my opponents' allegedly unequal advantages.

Interests Defended by Power

All groups use their power to defend their interests — but some have more power, some less. The great social gospel leader Walter Rauschenbusch wrote: " The strong have power to defend their just interests, and usually enough left over to defend their unjust interests too."

But to the strong, all their own interests appear to be just, and their use of power to defend all those interests appears to be justified.

Those who have different interests and different ideas of what is just must either organize the power to balance them or give in.

The points we have been making here are the ones which that nonpolitical American attitude we talked about back in Chapter 1 tends to overlook. It fails to recognize life's fundamental conflicts of interest; it does not see how deeply group interests affect everyone's reasoning; it overlooks the reality and importance of disproportions of power. Put these all together and they spell "idealist," the frame of mind especially prevalent in church circles.

But in the church's own teaching there is solid ground for quite another frame of mind. We began this chapter with a reference to man's sinful nature. If we do begin with that understanding of man's willful turning toward himself, then the idealist's picture of society fades away. In place of the stable, harmonious, "normal" world in which men's interests fit together, reason and conscience can prevail, and war and political struggle are just occasional unfortunate aberrations caused by a few bad people, there appears quite another world: a world in which all men are struggling for self-justification, through power, or wealth, or prestige, or moral and spiritual pride — a world in which the struggle for power is endless, and no man is to be trusted with unchecked power.

Man's Conscience

But what we have said so far is only half the story. That volleyball *did* land on one side or another of the line. There is a truth in the matter.

Moreover, it is possible to play volleyball without an umpire. Persons do, on occasion, admit a truth against their interest.

This illustration suggests two points: first, that "interest" is not automatically bad; second, that there is more to political life than "interests."

The desires to protect oneself, one's family, one's status, one's economic group, region, and nation are, of course, not evil in themselves. Quite the contrary; they are real obligations. They become destructive, however, very quickly — more quickly than we ordinarily admit. In fact, noble motives at one level have evil effects at another: a worthy devotion to the interests of his family may make a man more ruthless in the competition for advancement in his job; an unselfish devotion to the nation's interest may make a man more fiercely opposed to that of other nations.

But " sin " as self-interest is not the whole of the picture. We are creatures not only of interests, but also of reason and conscience, and we are capable to some limited extent of standing aside and looking at ourselves as we are. We are not only sinful but we have implanted within us a memory of what righteousness is; we cannot quite forget. In fact, *our defensive attempts to justify our position betray our uneasy conscience; they show that, in a sense, we " know better."* The Christian view of man is that we are " fallen," and a " fall " must be from some *height:* it is *both* more negative and more positive than secular views of man. Because more is expected, and known to be possible, therefore the criticism is deeper and more thoroughgoing. Christianity knows both the grandeur and the misery of man, and the two go together.

It is important to see both parts of this duality. Often what happens is that when a simple optimism about the ability of reason and good will to prevail is destroyed, a simple pessimism takes its place.

All of us would like to justify our own position. One way to do that is to assume that we are entirely right and just, and that all opposing positions are untrue and wrong. But, when that is not possible, and we must admit to bias, then we may switch completely over to an opposite position. In a way it is the other side of the same coin. We may then say that since every position is biased anyway, and all anybody ever does is just to seek his own interest, we might as well just go ahead and look out for number one.

But faith stands at least as much against cynicism as against idealistic illusions. The Christian can never picture politics as simply a brute conflict of raw interests. As there is always a measure of sin still to be overcome in every position, so there is always a higher possibility for reason and conscience in every situation.

HALF A LOAF, HISTORY, AND HYDROGEN BOMBS

At an American youth conference (any youth conference) the speaker finishes his powerful address on "The Crisis of Our Time," sits on the platform before a hushed audience and waits, mopping his brow. There is "time for just a few questions." After a moment's pause, toward the rear of the auditorium one brave hand is raised. "What you have told us is all very interesting," says the young American, "but what can we *do* about it?"

The question represents at once both what is mistaken, and what is healthy, in our attitude toward society and history.

It represents, on the one hand, a naïve inclination to try to meet enormously complex forces with some one decisive solution that we can effect, say, in the next hour and a half.

It represents, on the other, a healthy inclination to relate ourselves productively to the tasks that history poses.

What we must do is to hold to the latter and get rid of the former; to unite American idealism and vitality with greater wisdom, depth, maturity, steadfastness.

This may be where the Christian tradition comes in.

Having been around a long time, Christianity has gathered into itself a great deal of mature wisdom about the complicated way that history moves along. The belief in a judging and forgiving God who stands beyond all these human enterprises should introduce a certain modesty about the finality or goodness of any of them. It should bring a greater sense of the immensity and variety of this human drama, and of the tangle of good and evil that runs all the way through it. Evil does not have one address, like Moscow, or just one instrument, like war, communism, private property, or faulty education. Rooted in man himself, the evils of social life reappear in constantly changing forms; each revolutionary effort to eradicate them itself brings new and unlooked-for examples of the very evils it tried to do away with. Men are men, not gods, and they are neither so powerful that they can control history nor so good that the results would be pretty if they could.

We Can't Do Everything

Christianity's wisdom about history may contribute a sense of the limits on what can be done that the activist and idealist American (" What can we *do* about it? ") often lacks.

C. B. Marshall, who used to be with the State Department, said that the idealistic American is like the cheerleader. He stays on the side lines and yells, " We want a touchdown " (peace, justice, welfare), but he doesn't really know what it takes to get it, nor does he have to make the decisions. The policy maker, on the other hand, is like the quarterback, who is actually on the field, who has to make the decisions concretely, and who must therefore have a realistic sense of how much to try for, and when. He knows that the *timing* of what we do is important. What works at one time will not work at another, and the time at which a thing is done is almost as important as what is done. There must be a *readiness* for change in order for it to fit into history without causing more trouble than the gains it makes.

The policy maker must also be aware of *the cost of change*. He knows that he has to give up something, the surprise of a play, the energy of the fullback, time in the quarter, in return for his gains. The cheerleader rarely pays much attention to the cost.

The policy maker is aware that values are limited, and that they seem to have a certain mutual exclusiveness. Therefore, he is more attentive to seeing what one is giving up in return for what one is getting. He looks at budgets. It's all very nice, he says, to imagine a Utopia, but the resources to create it are limited and need to be husbanded with care.

He should also be aware of *the unintended consequences* of action. We cannot completely predict what will result from our plans. We may get other results than those which we project: an interception, a fumble, or even, having attained the gain that we wanted, a shift on the playing field so that we can't play for a field goal. Many reformers are unaware that their plans will have somewhat different results, when put into action, than they seem to have in the blueprint stage.

So the lessons here are: beware of abstract ideals, unrelated to the context in which they will be realized; look to the cost and possible consequences other than those you want; beware of sweeping claims for panaceas and utopias; don't begin with some ideal scheme, but begin instead with the possibilities of the real world.

The limits upon man's ability to control history are not just the limitation of resources; they are also the limits *in man*. In the last chapter we talked about man's sinfulness, but man is limited in more ways than that. Men are born into families and nations, with brothers and sisters and compatriots, into races and traditions, with characteristics that become part of them and cannot be wished away in a moment.

A sociologist writes of that modern " progressive " feeling

that it would be nice to raise children with the training of many religions so that after coming of age they can "pick their own." Why not, he asks, do the same for the name of the child? Think of the arbitrariness of having "Jimmy" or "Sally" slapped on the innocent baby without the ability to choose! This reduction to absurdity drives home the irreducible feature of the given elements, not only the natural ones, but also those which *grow,* the traditional and habitual ways of doing things.

There is the limit of what the human brain can do and know. The concluding sentence of a study of an attempt at planning — the planning and building of aircraft in wartime Britain — says, "Those who are best at planning and co-ordination . . . are those who realize that complete over-all planning and co-ordination by one directorate is quite impossible."

There are limits on social change, too, in the irrational elements of man and society. Men have habits and preferences that don't make sense but that are real anyway. They have loves and hates and symbols and notions and myths which reason may find hollow but which the social policy had better pay attention to, anyway. Men like the old schoolhouse the way it was, and they weep for the flag, and they honor what has been honored, and change their habits not all at once, as a result of reasoning, but over time, as a result of growth.

Man cannot ignore the imponderables of history, and the particular, given, and irrational, elements of life.

This element in Christian faith — the recognition of our limitations — turns us always toward the real world, with its real complexities and difficulties. Eric Hoffer states that radicals and reactionaries are alike in that they both despise reality. But the Christian does not despise reality. He does not begin with a blueprint that the world should be made to fit. He begins rather with the given world. Kierkegaard once said that God in relation to man is like a capitalist with an improvident debtor: he would rather have what payment he can get today than promises of full payment tomorrow. So God would have us effect what measure of justice we can achieve in this real world today, rather than utopian promises of some full justice which we will effectuate tomorrow.

We Can Do Something

But the Christian awareness of reality does not need to be a kind of wet blanket on human hopes, a constant counsel of despair about anything we try to do. Quite the contrary. Christians, waiting upon the Lord, are supposed to renew their strength, run and not be weary, walk and not faint. The realistic faith is supposed to be a source of a greater human vitality and a stronger human purpose. Why? Because in it we do not need to fool ourselves in order to act. We do not need to convince ourselves that we have the whole truth, or that our aims will inevitably triumph. Our hope rests not in our own power or virtue, or in expectations that things will automatically get better tomorrow, but rather beyond history, in a Creator who faints not. We do what we can, and the rest is in his hands.

And then, what we can do sometimes (not always) turns out to be not so insignificant after all.

The H-bomb War

The most obvious place to apply what we have been saying is in world politics. The constant fault of the American public is to expect too much: to ignore the limits, and then to be disillusioned. At first, World War I was no business of ours, a European squabble; then it was a war to end war, a war to make the world safe for democracy. Afterward, there was a great disillusionment, and that disillusionment contributed to our unrealistic and isolationist response to the rise of the dictators in the '30's — our failure to do even what we could have done.

The result of ignoring the limits of history is to expect total solutions — complete, certain, final — and to be dissatisfied with anything short of that. But all action in history is partial and full of risk, bringing new problems as it begins to settle the old.

The response of the public to the Korean War is the clearest and most important example of what we are saying about American attitudes. The United States performed a remarkable historical role in the United Nations action in Korea. But as the war went on, more and more Americans became angry at this " limited " war. The war, unanimously supported at its start, soon became a subject of partisan efforts to obtain votes. Why? Because it represented something incomprehensible. Here was a war that wasn't a war, a " limited war," a " police action "; it was a war that was fought, and yet could not be fought with all the means at our disposal. We were in it, and it drained us of men and money, yet we could not do everything that was possible to win it. This frustrating combination was foreign to the American mind, with its desire for total solution. Either win it, we said, or get out.

But the Korean War symbolizes exactly what we must have the stamina to do in the nuclear age: to resist, yet within limits. We have the appalling task of opposing the twin horrors of the twentieth century, the totalitarian police state and thermonuclear war. No situation could illustrate more dramatically what we said back in Chapter 3, that we deal not with one isolated moral principle set over against unprinciple, but rather with a clash of principles. To isolate a single moral absolute — either against the H-bomb or against communism — would be wrong, for we face both evils, and others besides. What we need is not the passionate crusading "righteous" spirit Americans so yearn to fall into, but a most careful, restrained, clearheaded and qualified effort to find what we can do within the limits history provides for us now. Action for *limited* objectives, to restrain communist expansion without precipitating the nuclear holocaust, is surely part of the program we need the moral discipline to sustain.

The nuclear age needs calm thought, and, given that, can yield some insight into what we can " do about it." We cannot, as the impulsive desire for total solutions urges us to do, wipe away the whole problem by banning the bomb in formal disarmament agreements with the Russians. Disarmament realistically can only follow, it cannot precede, the resolution of the political tensions that produce the arms, and the unpolitical effort to strike straight for some abolition of the bomb may play into the hands of the Russians' propaganda game. Neither can we wipe out the problem by the other worst course of all, initiating all-out war ourselves. The continuing impulse toward "preventive war" must be resisted by all who are morally earnest.

But, if we recognize that we cannot remove the risks and problems of life in this age, and if instead we confront them patiently, we may find some steps we can take. The existence of nuclear weapons may cause a kind of tacit understanding with the Soviets that is stronger than any formal agreement on paper could be. This tacit mutual understanding, that neither one of us wants world suicide, may leave room for us to contend in other ways. What we should do is to provide ourselves as many alternatives as possible, short of world suicide, within which that contention may take place.

Against those who overemphasize the sheer military contest,

we must see that the primary battle will be the economic-political-ideological struggle for the allegiance of the uncommitted nations of the world, and that as in this fight the weapons of the communists are diverse, so must our part be many-sided, with the economic perhaps the foremost.

We must be prepared to fight on a limited scale, for limited purposes, if possible without using nuclear weapons. The appalling danger of America's heavy reliance on the biggest nuclear weapons is that we may, when the communists make continuing small advances, leave ourselves stuck with the choice of surrender or suicide. We must provide ourselves "conventional" military capabilities, so that we can resist communist advances without destroying humanity.

The chief point of our discussion is that an all-or-nothing mind is a kind of irresponsible luxury. With the responsibilities of the present we Americans must bear the risks and the costs of the endless effort to do as much as we can where we are with the situation as it is. That's "what we can do about it."

Our ablity to do that depends in great part on the quality of political life in our own democracy. So we turn to that subject in the next two chapters.

CONVICTION, COMPROMISE, AND THE CROWD

Democracy is a great and wonderful instrument; we who have never been deprived of its virtues probably do not sufficiently appreciate it. But it is also a hard and even a dangerous instrument, and we probably don't sufficiently appreciate that, either.

The difficulties and dangers of democracy are inherent in the features that make it great; therefore, we must constantly confront and deal with them.

The two chief defining elements of democracy — majority rule and individual rights — are among the greatest social achievements of mankind; but they also both have within them the possibility of irresponsibility. Either one, or both together, can lead to an elaborate and endless passing of the buck.

The majority-rule people may say, " Shucks, everybody is doing it " or, " We give the public what it wants."

The individual-rights people may say, " Well, it's a free country, isn't it? "

A Word Against the Crowd

Many (perhaps most) Christians of the past have not been enthusiastic about democracy. For example, that Danish Christian writer whom the theologians are now always quoting, Sören Kierkegaard, did not like it a bit; he wrote in his *Journal*: "These democrats are so opposed to monarchy that they even want four-part solos!" Kierkegaard did not know and appreciate democracy as we do and he was concerned with the religious and ethical dimension only, not with the political. What he wrote nevertheless applies in part to politics. He wrote: The *crowd* is *untruth*. By this he did not mean anything so snobbish as the peasant, the poor, or some allegedly lower order of persons; rather he meant by "the crowd" any group that takes numbers as having decisive significance for truth. The same is true with a crowd of millionaires, noblemen, or laymen theologians. Number does not make truth. Kierkegaard told a story about a tavern keeper who bought drinks at five pennies apiece, sold them for three. "How do you make anything?" he was asked. "Oh, it's the volume!" he said.

The point is: no "volume," no number, makes truth or goodness or responsibility, if each individual unit lacks it.

No number of those who are unwise gives wisdom.

No number of irresponsible persons gives responsibility.

And democracy (misunderstood) may encourage a giving-up of the effort to be wise and responsible.

You know how it is with a certain kind of feeling of "democracy": nobody does it; everybody does it. Everybody blames what happens on everybody else. The crowd as a whole does it; no individual himself takes the responsibility for what happens.

The Congressmen often just reflects the lowest level of common interests and prejudices of his local district, without qualifying it by his own conviction and leadership and without relating that local interest to the good of the nation and the world.

The operator of the television network or the motion-picture studio justifies the material he puts out by saying, "We give the public what it wants." That is only half true, and half a denial of his own responsibility. He helps to determine what the public wants, and he picks from among the many things the public may want what he wants to give them — what is easiest, quickest, most superficial and profitable.

The citizen, lost in the mass, stops having convictions of his own, stops reading and working to find what is true and right, and takes what his neighbors say.

The crowd is untruth, said Kierkegaard, because by its very nature it renders the individual *irresponsible* and *impenitent*.

Lord Bryce noticed in this country a "fatalism of the multitude," and gave an example that we have all experienced: the feeling of a voter after his candidate has been defeated in an election. After such a defeat, "the average man will repeat his arguments with less faith, less zeal, more of a secret feeling that he may be wrong."

Although one may not agree with him on the issue or other points, one cannot help having a certain respect for the posture that columnist Sokolsky struck in 1948 after Mr. Truman, whom he had opposed, was elected. Someone chided Mr. Sokolsky for being wrong. "I wasn't wrong," he said; "the people were wrong."

The point is not that we should determine our opinions either by accepting or rejecting what people say: it is rather that we should have convictions founded on our own thought and conscience.

The word "democracy" is often used to imply that some mystical truth and goodness will come out of the sheer fact of people being together and talking and voting. But it doesn't.

Personal responsibility is endangered by a sloppy spirit of democracy; yet that personal responsibility is necessary for democracy itself truly to function. If persons, one by one, do not take responsibility, then the people as a whole will not really prevail.

The clear and present danger of the democratic spirit is that the valuable democratic truth, that it is right that the people rule, may lead to the populistic half-truth, that the majority ("the people") *will* rule what is right (they won't necessarily); and this, in turn, may lead to the relativistic falsehood, that there is no right except what the majority rules, that is, that there really is no such thing as right or good at all, but just desire, opinion, interest.

We have said many words in this book against the corruption in American Protestantism, of an overdone individualism. Let's now just say this good word for it: the Protestant spirit, at its best, has taught (and nowhere more than in America) the personal responsibility, the claim upon the individual will, without which democracy doesn't work. We need more of the Protestant spirit, in that sense, today.

A Word for the People

But then, of course, many individuals manage to be irresponsible and impenitent without any help from the crowd.

And many crusty individualists, perhaps like Mr. Sokolsky, who agree with our first point (that majorities don't make truth) miss the second point: that unrestrained individual opinion, even when it is "thoughtful," doesn't get full truth (or justice) either. Why not? Look back at Chapter 6; all ideas of "justice" are colored by the particular background and group interest of the one holding the idea. You from the North don't *really* know what it's like to be a Southern white. And the Southern white doesn't *really* know what it's like to be a Southern Negro.

So now let's say this good word for democratic procedures: they mean, when they work right, that every group's interest and opinion has to be attended to. And that's good.

The principle of majority rule is important because it is the reflection in politics of the equality of men before God. All forms of minority rule rest on inequality. Majority rule insures that in one place at least, in the control of the instrument of legitimate force, the government, men shall stand, as they stand before God, as equals.

God's love is not " equal " in the sense that we are all a row of equally loved souls, included like ciphers under the general proposition that God loves everybody. But in earthly power, where the increase of one man may well mean the diminishing of another, the best representation of that ultimate equality is the equality of one equals one, of majorities. God takes account of the unique personality; the ballot box does not, and that's just as well.

The Christian point of view means that a man knows his own group's ideas are incomplete and even warped; therefore he not only *accepts,* he should welcome and desire, the restraint upon and enlargement of his own perspective by the perspective of others. That's what democracy does: it does not necessarily get at truth and goodness; it does insure that each group's idea of truth and goodness (and each group's interest) will be both attended to and limited by the power of other groups.

Since all our conceptions of what is right and just are influenced by our interests, it is good that we are forced to mitigate our claims by the pressure of other opposing definitions of what is right and just, colored by other interests. It is good that there is " compromise " between the claims of employer and employee, producer and consumer, farmer and cityfolk, old stock and immigrant, taxpayer and government beneficiary. It is good that none of these prevail without the pressure to compromise with others. Majority rule — the rule of the people — helps to insure that pressure.

But, still, the democrat has the hard job of holding together two principles, which falsely understood may tend to destroy each other, that majorities should rule, and that what is true and good is independent of majorities.

The people will not necessarily choose what is right. The voice of the people is not the voice of God.

Sometimes Americans are shocked to learn that their Puritan forefathers, who did not believe in the sovereignty of kings, of bishops, of nobles, *also* did not believe in the sovereignty of the people. They believed in the sovereignty of God.

They were wrong in letting the New England clergy think it could speak finally for God's sovereignty. They were wrong in not seeing that democracy is the best earthly method for checking each group's tendency to confuse itself with the Almighty, and for finding a justice and a common good. But they were right that the people, the majority, is not the final arbiter of truth.

POLICIES, PERSONALITIES, AND PARTIES

Morally earnest Americans often say that they are *independent* in politics, and not tied to any party: "I don't vote a straight party ticket, the way a party tells me to; I vote my honest convictions." The implication seems to be that conscientious citizenship necessarily requires independence of political parties, and that independence is morally superior to party allegiance. But it is not.

There are, of course, many different positions that Christians may, and do, take in American politics. These include allegiance to one of the major parties (Republican or Democratic), independence of any party, allegiance to a minor party (Socialist or Progressive), or even good old-fashioned apathy. All of these have their place.

Take apathy, for instance. Possibly it serves a purpose that there are some people who are concerned more with writing a poem or making a million dollars or losing twenty pounds or other such triumphs of the human spirit than they are with politics. These apathetics may keep the total temperature from going too high, and play a certain role in the total economy of God. However, we are not recommending that position. There is a sufficient supply of apathy without anybody's trying for it.

What position are we recommending? Let's call it *critical partisanship*.

We want to argue a bit, in this chapter, with the familiar desire for "independent" citizens and "independent" candidates, because this desire is often an illustration of the nonpolitical attitude, rife among American Protestants, that this book has criticized.

Sometimes the independent seems to be heading for that moral island we talked about in Chapter 3, keeping himself "pure and unspotted," rather than trying to affect the world; he often reflects an attitude that is unaware of concrete issues, of power, of policy, of the need for organization and compromise.

No Personality Contest

The lady who wanted Governor Dewey to be president because it would be nice to have a President with a mustache, and the other lady who opposed him because he looked like the bridegroom on a wedding cake, should both be discouraged. So should the people who were enthusiastic about Governor Stevenson because he wore button-down collars on his shirts, or enthusiastic about General Ike because of his grin. And there are much more subtle forms of this personal, extrapolitical appeal to independents. The Protestant community in America is especially susceptible, as we have said, to appeals based on the "morality" or "integrity" or "sincerity" or "respectability" of the candidate or group, without noticing how these phrases may cloak certain class and group prejudices, and leave policy questions unexamined. But politics is not a personality contest. The question is, rather, which values and interests will prevail.

What's "Efficient" Depends on Where You Sit

Independents are also given to voting for "honesty and efficiency," which undeniably are great virtues, but such voters assume that the prior question (what is it we are going to be "honest and efficient" in doing) is settled. In business, it may be; in politics, it usually isn't.

"Efficiency" means giving up the least value to obtain the most value; it means, no *waste* of valuable things like time, money, resources. But what's efficient depends on what is counted as valuable: one man's "efficiency" is another man's poison. It is efficient for the business to dump its sludge in the river; it is *not* efficient for the community as a whole.

In this very practical technical society, this American land of know-how, we need to insist that you have to know *why* and *what* before knowing how is of any use. The overwhelming emphasis on the practical and technical tends to squeeze out consideration of goals, ends, values, policies, ideas: it overlooks the fact that the how often implicitly smuggles in its own too-simple answer to these questions.

I wonder how a book would sell, entitled *How to Get Over HOW–TO–ISM;* the *KNOW–HOW* of *KNOWING* more than *HOW;* A Practical Guide to Overcoming Excessive Practicality, in three easy, simple steps.

Step one. Don't expect to accomplish anything very important in three easy simple steps.

Step two. Tell yourself every day that there is nothing more impractical than life lived wholly at the level of the practical.

Step three. Remember that, though great truths may be simple, if you always head straight for what is simple, you won't get very much truth.

Government is not merely a realm of "efficient" administration. Government is not like business, for in government resides the power that decides about justice in the community. Those independents who seem to say that all we need to do is vote for the clean-shaven candidates who keep their desks clear have missed the point: politics is fundamentally about policy.

But, you may say, that's not the kind of independence we mean: we mean a thoughtful independence that *is* concerned with policy, and that doesn't want the vested interest of parties to get in the way. You have a point.

Down with Thoughtless Partisanship

Much party allegiance has no better basis than that pappy and grandpappy were Democrats (or Republicans) or that all the men at the office are Republicans (or Democrats). Much of the partisanship at the ward meeting has more to do with patronage, personal careers, and ethnic and other group rivalries than it does with the issues of the day. These considerations are not wholly to be disdained: the parties have played an important role, for example, in giving successive waves of immigration concrete help, an opportunity for advancement, a feeling of belonging. However, these aspects are becoming a lesser ingredient in the political stew. Insofar as the independent wants to decrease their importance, and increase that of thought about issues, he can do a service. That, in fact, is just what we mean by the word " critical " in our phrase " critical partisanship."

Parties Are Significant

Why not, then, just be critical?

Why bother with the party?

The political process is much more than voting. The shaping of issues, the dispensing of patronage, and the selecting of candidates are very important, and they all center around the parties. For the citizen to have a responsible relationship to these basic features of politics he must be related to one of the major party organizations.

Even in voting, party affiliation is more important than is sometimes recognized. The idea that "there are no real differences between the parties" is a cliché of the man who hasn't gone into it very much. Of course, neither party is *purely* one thing or other — and that, by the way, is a good thing! It's the *proportions* that count, and they *do* differ significantly. The parties have different histories, different constituencies, a different balance of different kinds of left and right. Look at the proportions. Then work within the party nearest you for what you think should be done.

That means compromise? Fine! Look at it this way: We said in the last chapter that it is good that there is compromise between competing claims. It is here that the party may play a valuable role. Major parties, since they must seek a majority, must make some amalgamation of a variety of interests in the community. They cannot afford to become the agent of simply one group, however large. The Republican Party cannot afford to be simply the business party, but must bid successfully for other votes. The Democratic Party cannot be simply a labor party, but must bid for the votes of others in the community. This necessity to seek a majority forces the major parties to shave off some of the extremes of the claims of the different interest groups, and it puts some pressure on them (not enough, unfortunately) to fit together the various claims into an over-all program.

The party's effort to *win* means you have to pay attention to those folks on the other side of the tracks, to groups and interests and positions you otherwise could ignore.

You say the party as you've seen it isn't too attractive? Well, leaven it! And be leavened a bit in return!

But aren't these principles that we should not compromise at all? Aren't there times when the whole society — all parties — are going in the wrong direction? Yes, indeed — Nazi Germany, for an obvious example. But do you really think the American party system is in that situation? Often the "plague on both your houses" attitude of the idealistic Protestant springs more from his own inner need to be pure and radical than from an objective analysis of the situation.

Finally, the party represents the *organization* that ideals require in order to become realities.

The Protestant idealism of which we have spoken tends to underestimate the importance of organization. Some Protestants, like a famous liberal Senator, seem to feel that they have corrupted their principles if they find that more than two or three other people agree with them. Certainly it is true, on the other hand, that most American Protestants are in plenty of organizations — too many, perhaps. What we need is a greater appreciation of the type of organization that has access to the channels of power in the society. The hard work to organize a great majority of the people has its genuine moral stature. Indeed, the man who compromises, up to a point, in order to achieve his ideals in the real world may be more "moral" than the man who preserves them intact in defeat and isolation.

CHAPTER 10

A CONCLUSION

The trouble with the politics of many Christians is not that they aren't Christian enough; it's that they aren't political enough.

Many good Christians, aware of the sin of man as they should be, knowing the ambiguity of history as they should know it, trusting in the purposes of God that transcend our purposes as they should trust them, seeking the never-completed justice of the ever-coming Kingdom of God as they should seek it, able to give the most theological basis for politics, able, too, to bring the most worthy and generous motives to bear on questions of the day — many such Christians still don't help much, when it comes right down to the questions of justice that abound in day-to-day politics.

Why? Because they don't know what they are talking about.

There is no substitute for reading about what's going on.

Even more important, there is no substitute for having participated in the actualities of politics . . . or for having reflected a bit on the politics in which we all, one way or another, have participated. When you've tried to get a resolution passed or a candidate elected in some conglomerate body of disparate interests and desires, when you've been through the caucuses and seen the necessities — and the dangers — of compromise, and the necessities — and the dangers — of ideals, when you have dealt with the varieties of opinion and interest, learned the usefulness and the pervasiveness of power, tried to translate some program from a dream into an actuality through the difficult hurdles of politics, then you are able to look upon the politics of the larger scene with different and more discerning eyes.

You see then that the politics of everyday must be a matter of rough proportions, not of pure values, of continual half loaves and compromise that, nevertheless, in their reality are better than the imagined goal. You see then, as Winston Churchill wrote about the moment of his coming to power as Prime Minister in the dark hours of the war, that "facts are better than dreams."

You are then able to know something of the way that dreams are made into facts.

Living Our Faith

There surely is in our faith a ground and motive for this concrete wisdom which comes through reflection on our participation in the affairs of the real world. Perhaps it's found in this: that we do not have a philosophy of life with God as an abstract principle from which other principles are derived; rather we hold to a faith in a living God to whose action we respond with our action. We do not have a theory from which we derive right positions; we have a relationship in which a dialogue is continually carried on about what might be the right positions. We do not have "Christian" principles for politics; we have a Christian dimension to our living in politics.

We do not have answers; we have a reason — a personal reason — for continually seeking answers.

Therefore the theory — even the erudite and historic theological theory — is incomplete without the living participation
of particular Christians who are willing to be active in particular political situations.

Like all the rest of Christian faith, the Christian's political
faith is really seen not in abstractions or institutions but in
the living of it.